How to Shoot Better than Stephen Curry

The Ultimate Guide to Better Basketball Shooting

Aaron Atlas

Text copyright © 2016 Aaron Atlas
All Rights Reserved

Disclaimer: No part of this publication may be reproduced or transmitted in any form or by any means, or transmitted electronically without direct written permission in writing from the author.

While all attempts have been made to verify the information provided in this publication, neither the author nor the publisher assumes any responsibility for errors, omissions, or misuse of the subject matter contained in this book.

This book is for entertainment purposes only, and the views expressed are those of the author alone, and should not be taken as expert instruction. The reader is responsible for their own actions.

Adherence to applicable laws and regulations, including international, federal, state and local governing professional licensing business practices, advertising and all other aspects of doing business in the U.S.A., Canada or any other jurisdiction is the sole responsibility of the purchaser or reader.

This Book is dedicated to all the Hoopers from Indiana who had the talent, skill and heart, but never made it to the NBA. And to all those who were overlooked, just like Stephen Curry.

Special Offer from the Author

Thank you for buying this book. It means that you are serious about your game and improving your shooting skills. As a gift and a special bonus for all those who buy this book, I am offering my coaching services to you at a deeply discounted rate. For just $20 US Dollars I will watch a five minute video of you shooting. I will write out a detailed summary and full analysis critiquing your form and telling your where to improve. I will also do a 25 minute Skype Coaching Session with you to show you exactly how to improve and to talk with you about your game in further detail.

To receive this Special Bonus send an email along with a video of your shooting form to onlinebasketballcoaching@gmail.com.

Table of Contents

Introduction

Chapter 1: My Basketball Journey

Chapter 2: The Indiana Basketball Tradition

Chapter 3: The Dominance of Stephen Curry

Chapter 4: The Importance of the Jump Shot

Chapter 5: Lower Body Mechanics

Chapter 6: Upper Body Mechanics

Chapter 7: The Stephen Curry Jump Shot

Chapter 8: Mindset

Chapter 9: Last Tips

Chapter 10: Closing Thoughts

Introduction

So, you have watched a few games of basketball on television. Now you want to go outside and emulate your favorite player on your driveway hoop without looking like a complete idiot. You want to be the next Stephen Curry.

Maybe you have watched more than just a few games of basketball on television.

Maybe you were born with a basketball in your hand and have dreams of playing one day in the NBA, the highest level of basketball in the world.

Regardless of your skill level or your aspirational level, this book is for you!

First off, earning a college scholarship in any sport is hard. There are a lot of factors that go into earning an athletic scholarship, many of them outside of your control. Let me just address of a few of those factors for you:

1. You don't have the money to attend all the best camps in the country to gain the skills necessary to develop into and compete with the best players

2. You don't have the money to play on the best travel teams that have the best coaches, play the best teams and earn the most exposure at national tournaments

3. You don't have the best coaches at your school that not only can teach you and turn you into the best player, but they do not

have the network, contacts or marketing skills to get you known to college scouts and programs

4. You do not play in a state, area or conference where there is high level talent and both you and your school is not on the radar of any college scouts

5. Your coach, parents and teachers are not supportive of your passion and dreams and you face an uphill battle in your pursuit of athletic glory

6. Your grades are below par when it comes to being ready for college and many schools, particularly smaller schools that can only offer academic scholarships and not athletic scholarships, cannot display interest

There are several other factors that go into earning a college scholarship and playing college basketball, but those are just some of the factors that may be outside of your control. So while you may want to think about some of these factors and figure out a way to get past them if you are facing them, you want to focus your attention on what you can control.

And now, with this book and the information that it contains, you will be able to control the type of jump shot you possess. You will have a jump shot that will be college ready and, maybe if you practice and perfect it enough, NBA ready. And just like Stephen Curry, it will be a sight to behold!

Now, let me ask you a few simple questions.

Do you want to be picked first on the blacktop at the park?

Do you want to avoid being made fun of by other kids who are more athletic and naturally talented?

Do you want to earn a college scholarship to a division 1 school with tons of media and television publicity?

Do you want to earn a living as a professional basketball player on the grandest stage of sports just like Stephen Curry?

Those questions seemed pretty easy, huh? You should have answered yes to all those questions. But more so, with this e-book you can literally go from being the worst kid in your school to being the best player in your state by following the information that is in this book. I know this is true because my very own brother did it without having this book to help him!

Getting a better shot is more than just about scoring more points on the court. It will give you the confidence to score more points off the court too: on tests, with girls and in life. Having a million dollar jump shot just like Stephen Curry is almost on the level of having a million dollar smile, a million dollar handshake and a million dollar wardrobe. Sounds awesome, huh?

So, let's get started! This book is going to give you the tools, skills, principles, fundamentals, mindset and confidence to shoot better than Stephen Curry!

Chapter 1: My Basketball Journey

My name is Aaron Atlas. I am originally from the Hoosier state of Indiana where I grew up playing basketball at an early age. Well, in Indiana terms, I actually started playing at a later age. I was about 11 years old when I first started playing organized basketball.

I actually started out playing t-ball and then graduated to playing kickball at recess. My mother got me into bowling when I was little and also a little putt-putt during the summer months. I was very good at both, so I guess I naturally had great hand-eye coordination which would come in handy in my basketball pursuits.

My brother and I grew up as only siblings and had to play together when we were young. We were known as the baseball brothers. We would be in our backyard for hours just throwing the ball back and forth. We were really good. Yet, although baseball was fun for us, Indiana was a basketball state.

I was too poor to ever own a basketball, let alone have a basketball goal in my driveway, but thankfully I grew up on a block where I had friends my age that had basketball goals in their driveway. We would play for hours and then play some more at recess (whenever we needed a little break from all the kickball action).

Thankfully, both of my friends had dads who taught them a little (or a lot) about basketball. They knew how to dribble, pass and shoot the ball. They knew how to stand, where to stand and even how to keep track of the score. I really wasn't that good and had no idea what I was doing, but I guess they preferred to have someone around they could beat up on. I guess that is more fun than just always shooting around by yourself. So I found myself playing in their driveways often, honing my skills while getting beat pretty bad.

Our small city had an elementary basketball league and our school was holding tryouts. Most of the guys, including many of my close friends, were going out for the team. Along with my brother, I made the team and the rest is history.

Well sort of. My fifth grade year I was one of the last players to make the team. In fact, my twin brother was the last one to make the team. Although my brother barely made the team his fifth grade year, he practiced all summer long in the driveway, with just a $5 pizza hut basketball and no basket; just him, the ball, the sidewalk and a lot of heart. He came back the next year to be the best player in our city and by his 7th grade year, he was arguably one of the best players in our state.

But my brother was a point guard and his shot was definitely not the best. It wasn't until after he stopped playing in high school and went to college that he perfected his stroke. He then became the best player on the court no matter where he played, essentially hitting almost every shot he took, including running one foot three pointers on the fast break (which is not very fundamentally sound and I do not recommend).

But back to my elementary school playing days. First game of the year, I was a substitute on the bench and only played just a few minutes of the game. But during those few short minutes I made a layup (which is how most points are scored during an elementary game) and I was fouled twice and hit all four of my free throws.

I wasn't the tallest kid on the court. I certainly was not the strongest, nor the fastest. My shot wasn't the best either, but I made four free throws. I hit 100% of my shots in the game and became the third leading scorer on my team that game. I immediately went from being a substitute on the bench, not even knowing if I was going to play, to becoming a starter for every game the rest of the season.

The reality is that I never even scored another point the entire season until the playoffs, but because I made those free throws and had a nice looking shot, I was a starter who could do no wrong in the eyes of my coach. I was a player who could become hot at any time.

Thankfully, I had a coach in elementary who really believed in me and he instilled confidence in myself and our entire team. He was a dad of one of my friends. Most coaches at that time and at that level are usually fathers of one of the players. While he certainly helped his son a lot during the season, he also took the time to help develop every player on the team.

He is the one who taught me to love the game of basketball. But it wasn't until I made the local AAU team that I began to learn how to actually play organized basketball.

I had a coach who didn't have any children on the team. He was a younger guy. He played college basketball at a small school in my home state. He wasn't someone just volunteering their time because he wanted to help out his son, he was actually coaching because he was engrossed in the game of basketball.

My brother and I had just played on the elementary team that beat his team in the Final Four and went on to play in the championship game where we were just one last second shot away from winning. In fact, the team that ended up beating us in the championship game had earlier in the season came to our home court and killed us by more than 40 points. Yes, that is right. They beat us by 40 points. By the end of the season, we all were way better, both as a team and as individuals, and ended up only losing to them by 3 points.

My brother and I were the only players from our elementary team to actually play AAU. The strange thing was, we didn't even know about AAU. One of our team mates told us about the tryouts.

And this is when the story gets funny. So the AAU tryouts for this team, that was made up of all the best players from all the local elementary teams, were held on the same night as our local city-wide D.A.R.E. dance. Now, if there was one thing that got us more excited than basketball, it was definitely going to a dance, especially being the first dance where we would be able to see other girls from all the other elementary schools.

I think we talked more about the dance that night at school than we did about tryouts. In fact, tryouts were just an afterthought for me. I actually showed up a little late to the tryouts that night because I was so busy trying to get ready for the dance. I remember being in my bathroom at home worrying about my hair more so than how I was going to play that night at tryouts.

My mother was going to take my brother and I to the tryouts, then take us directly to the dance. I was in fifth grade. I was only 11 years old. I hadn't really hit puberty yet so I wasn't worried about sweating hard core at the tryouts, then going to the dance all gross and nasty. It just wasn't something that I had to worry about yet at that stage in my life.

So I roll up to tryouts wearing my nice shirt, my nice jean shorts and my hair combed, looking all spiff for the dance. I look around and all I see are the most serious basketball players I ever saw. They had all been there for at least 20 minutes to a half hour before me. They were all dribbling around, warming up, taking shots and looking good for the coaches who were watching from the sidelines.

They were already jockeying for a position on the team. They were showing their commitment, their hard work and their skills. We, on the other hand, came through the door and cared more about looking cool in front of all these other guys.

The only ones who cared about looking cooler than us, were my two friends who played on my elementary school team. They were there to tryout, but instead they were just sitting in the bleachers and watching.

I went up to them and asked them why they were not shooting around and they said that they were too old for the team. The AAU team was an 11 and under team and there was a cutoff for the age limit according to the state or national governing body.

My one friend had missed the birth date requirement by only a few months. I didn't know that at the time though. My friend was actually really tall for his age. He hit his growth spurt early and was already nearing 6 feet by the end of his fifth grade year. Because of that he was also hitting puberty. He was not only taller than everyone else in our city, but he had a deeper voice, he had some peach fuzz on his face and he had, he had…hair in his arm pits!

But more than just some kid who had an early growth spurt, he began telling everyone (even himself) that he was way older than he actually was. I remember him telling people that he was 13 for years. I guess it made him feel cooler, allowed him to hang out with guys who were much older and allowed him to talk to girls who were already in middle school and sometimes high school.

I think he mainly told people this (as well as himself) so that he could just feel normal. It had to be tough to walk into school every day and be the giant. It had to be hard to be the guy who everyone stared at, or was scared of.

So while my one friend was actually just a few months older than the cut off, meaning he still was just 11 years old, he walked in with my other friend who also had been telling kids for years he was much older than he was.

So when the head guy was checking in players and asking for their birth certificates to show proof of age, both of my friends lied to the guy and told him they were 13 and "way too old" to be playing with a bunch of 11 year olds.

So instead of trying out, they just sat in the stands. My brother and I were just happy to be able to play some basketball. We really didn't even want to make the team because our friends weren't eligible to play.

During tryouts we began to get to know some of the players and found out that a lot of the guys had been playing on this AAU team for years. Most of them all had dads who were coaches and who had paid for them to play.

While many of those players, mostly from the school that we had just beat in the Final Four, were all wealthy with nice shoes and nice basketball clothes on, we on the other hand, were poor and didn't really have a lot of fundamental training in basketball.

They all knew the proper way to shoot, to pass, to cut, to set a screen, to do a pick and roll, to play defense, to run drills and do what the coach was asking of them. I, on the other hand, was lost.

But my brother and I definitely stood out. Mainly it was because of our clothes. People thought we were pretty crazy to show up to basketball tryouts wearing party clothes. We also stood out because we were new to the team. Most of these players had been playing together for years, but we were the new kids on the block who had just been a part of a team that really shook the entire city to its core.

Before that season, our elementary school was always one of the weakest teams in the city. We were sort of a laughing stock in the basketball community. That year people really had low expectations of us as well. But when we only lost to two teams that season and stormed our way to the finals, losing just narrowly to the team who had earlier beat us by 40 points, was sort of a folk tale. We were urban legends in a sense.

We played a different style of basketball, a style that was rarely seen in these parts of the state, especially at a young age. It was a run and gun style of play. It was free flowing, attack the basket, use your speed and your athleticism to beat your opponents. Everyone else was playing slow down, work the ball around, set up a play, find the open man, take a high percentage shot style of play. And those were the type of coaches who were picking this AAU team.

But we stood out when it mattered most, during the end of practice scrimmage.

My brother and I were just out there playing loose and carefree. We didn't care about making the team. In fact, we thought there was no way we would make the team. Not because we weren't good enough, but because we didn't fit in. We weren't from the rich schools, we hadn't been playing for several years on the team, we didn't know all the drills and plays the coach was trying to run during the tryouts and we didn't come from money. We really weren't their style of players.

But our talent was hard to hide. We were playing more aggressive than the other players who were playing timid and nervous because they wanted to make the team. We were playing with more confidence than the others and it showed. We were getting steals. We were doing give and go plays to one another. We were scoring. And most importantly we were laughing and having fun.

We were mostly laughing because we didn't care about it. Everyone else cared a lot about making the team. We simply didn't. We were just so pumped and excited to get to that dance. We were thinking more about if they were going to play our favorite songs at the dance rather than if we were going to actually make the team.

Well, it turns out that we stood out enough to make the team. We were the only ones from my school, or any other lower income school, to make the team. Turns out that my coach was actually a twin himself. He liked our style of play, loved our confidence and saw a lot of himself and his twin brother in us. It was this twist of fate that led to our basketball dominance.

Our new coach was no slouch. He was tough, demanding and knew a lot about basketball. My brother and I didn't get much playing time that season, but just being on the bench and being in practice allowed us to learn so much more about the game.

He was a good coach of the game, teaching us the fundamentals and also about team basketball. In fact, his daughter just graduated high school as one of the best players in the nation. She led her team to a state final as a freshman point guard and ended up beating Damon Bailey's Bedford team, that starred Damon's daughter, for the state title her senior year in high school. She could have gone anywhere in the nation to play, but she chose to play at Notre Dame and follow in the footsteps of another Hoosier favorite Skylar Diggins of South Bend.

The next season when we played elementary again with my team mates who had not played AAU, it felt like we were on another level than them. I guess it didn't hurt that we finally got a little growth spurt and hit puberty as well. We went from being one of the smallest guys on the team to my brother playing center, while I played point guard at the same size.

We both dominated that season, going undefeated, winning the first ever Holiday tournament and going into the playoffs as the heavy favorite. Sadly, our over-confidence led to a second round loss and an early exit from the tournament.

But I ended up playing AAU on this team for four years, from my fifth grade year until my 8th grade year. During this time, we had great teams and we traveled all across the state of Indiana playing all the best players in the state. I got to guard these best players on a nightly basis and got to see up close the talent and skill of these players who would later go on to star for their high school and even play college ball. Some of them even went on to play in the NBA.

While I was one of, if not the fastest and most athletic players in the state while in middle school, I stopped growing in the 8th grade, allowing many other slower and less athletic guys to become taller and catch up to me a bit. While I was still the fastest, most athletic and one of the strongest guys in my high school, I realized that while I still had a good shot at playing college ball, it was now going to be a lot harder. Not many colleges are looking for 5 ft. 8 in. guards/power forwards in division 1.

I wasn't interested in playing small school ball. If I was going to play, I was going to play at the highest level. It didn't help that my high school coaches didn't have the highest character or the highest basketball acumen. I quit playing after my freshman year and our varsity team went on to win maybe three games a year each season while I was there.

The coaches had stolen the joy I had to play the game and I walked away. It wasn't until my brother got me to play when we went to Indiana University that I regained my love and passion for the game.

I hadn't really played ball for years. In fact, my skills and my shape were really rusty. I had gained more than just the freshman 15. I was up to about the freshman 20. I was spending all my time in my dorm room reading and studying for class and made no time to go to the gym.

Thankfully, my brother grabbed me one day after class and told me that we were going to go play basketball. I was so out of shape, I missed all my layups and I played horribly, but our team won every game and I had so much fun. I was so rusty, yet I was still playing really well against all these guys from all over the state and country who were attending the university with me.

As I was playing against all these guys, I was realizing after talking to them, that most of them had played basketball for their high school. Most of them had played varsity basketball, some of them had even played small division three college ball, but decided to transfer back to a larger school and focus on academics and just having fun. So I was playing against some of the best players in our state and consistently beating them, beating them bad.

By my sophomore year, my brother was arguably the best player on campus. And that included our school's basketball team.

One of the best stories I have ever witnessed while playing basketball came at the end of my freshman year at Indiana University. As usual, we were playing pick-up ball at the campus recreation facility. All of a sudden as we are playing on the court, we hear a lot of commotion on the sidelines. Lots of players were walking over to our court. I looked over and I saw one of the guys from the men's team on the sidelines and lots of people surrounding him.

At Indiana University, if you play on the basketball team you are a celebrity. Every student has your picture on a poster in their dorm room, every student has watched your games on television and live at Assembly Hall and every student knows all your stats and personal history. Every guy wants to be you and every girl wants to be with you.

Well, this player was the same year as us. We grew up playing basketball against him and never thought he was anything special. We knew he was the best player on his team, but we had seen lots of other players who were better.

But by his senior year in high school, this guy had not only grown to be 6 ft 3 inches, but he had an incredibly high vertical jump. He was definitely on a different level than he was while he was in middle school. In fact, one of the best in-game dunks I have ever seen was by this guy during his senior year in high school against one of our local high school teams.

It was a packed crowd at the 13th largest high school gymnasium in the country, a gymnasium that could hold over seven thousand fans. This player was all about the show.

He stole a ball right at midcourt and instead of rushing down the floor for a simple layup, he ended up waiting for the center of the opposing team, a guy who played small college ball before transferring to Indiana University himself, and slowly began his buildup towards the basket. The opposing center was on the left side of the court running full speed towards the basket to block the shot, while this player was slowly building up towards his ascent to the basket. As both players simultaneously got close to the basket and jumped in the air, this player who now played for IU flew in the air, turned his back towards the center and the basket and did a reverse two handed dunk while pulling himself up on the rim just a little bit to let the entire crowd know that he was the best on the floor.

He would later go on to compete in the McDonald's All-American slam dunk contest later that year in 2000 before he would attend Indiana University. But this wasn't high school basketball. This wasn't a high school showcase. This wasn't a game played with team jerseys, coaches and paying fans. This was the HPER, our much beloved rec center in the middle of our historic campus. And this was our court. He had to go through us.

We had already played a game or two and were pretty warmed up. This guy had picked up a squad he thought couldn't lose. They were all taller, bigger and stronger than our squad. They were more athletic and better than our squad, or so he thought.

As usual, he was confident and thought he would have a pretty easy game on his hands. After we went up 6-0, on a 15 point game, his attitude changed. He went from being nonchalant and carefree to being upset and frustrated with his team mates.

His team mates who were division 1 athletes, mostly on the football team, were all being out ran, out hustled and out muscled on every possession. We were dominating them. His team mates couldn't catch his pass without us intercepting it.

We purposely knew that the only person on that team who could do anything against us was this one guy. So we put our tallest guy on the team on him. Our tallest guy was actually a point guard and wasn't too physical at all. In fact, he was probably our weakest defender. But we figured if we put all our best defenders on the other players, we would lock them down and also be able to help off when this guy would drive.

We purposely let this guy score while shutting down the other players. This is a well-known strategy in basketball. He kept getting more and more upset as the game progressed. We were eventually up 14-7 and only needed one more point to win the game.

There he was on the court with what looked like a superior team getting beat by a bunch of short (we were all around 5 ft 8 inches except our tall guy who was 6 ft 3 but skinny and not very physical) guys in front of all these other guys in the gym who had come over just to watch him play.

This guy was not only a celebrity, but he was a budding star on the team. He started the season being a bench player as a freshman. One game he broke out with a 20 point effort and then became a regular in the rotation and even started a few games. As a freshman that was huge.

So as we went up 14-7 and on the verge of winning, he was mad and was determined to single handedly beat us. He had to. His other team mates were getting smoked and couldn't help him out. On top of that, he had dogged his team mates so much that they were upset with him and basically stopped playing offense because they knew he was no longer going to pass the ball.

This guy then sized up his opponent. He began dribbling the ball around the three point line and then aggressively drove down the middle of the lane right to the rack. He had to physically bulldog his way down the lane as two other guys helped off. But this guy was too big, too strong and could jump too high.

He made a layup right over the rim. But he was so frustrated by our speed and our quick transition game that after the ball went through the rim on this layup, he violently hit the ball down onto the next court. It was 14-8, this guy had just scored the last 7 points for his team, he was feeling confident and now had a little breathing room as he hit the ball down onto the other court to give him time to retreat on defense.

Well, he didn't know my brother. Sure we played against him when he was younger, but he wasn't that good then and we were on a different level at that time. We stopped playing in high school and he kept playing. He grew several inches and added several pounds of muscle while gaining tons of inches on his vertical jump. He was 6 ft 3, 205 lbs jumping close to a 40 inch vertical, maybe higher.

My brother was the same size he was as an eighth grader, 5 ft 8 (barely), 135 lbs with a 22 inch vertical (I am just guessing). My brother wasn't a high flyer. He was quick, he could hit any shot with anyone guarding him, he could steal the ball from anyone and he could make passes that people have never seen before.

In fact, if we would have put my brother on this guy he would have been even more frustrated and mad, because my brother would have picked him up full court and wouldn't have let him breath. He would have stolen the ball from him several times, but we let him have his space.

So there this guy was, retreating on defense with the ball rolling down towards the end of the other basketball court. My brother, one to never shy away from anybody or anything, ran as fast as he could onto the other court, picked up the ball and ran as fast as he could back onto our court.

Instead of passing the ball in, as is normal and the rule in basketball, my brother was not giving up the ball. This guy had disrespected the game and our team by hitting the ball onto the other court so my brother was going to disregard any other social norms of the game as well.

My brother ran onto our court without passing in the ball. The four other guys on this basketball player's team were still in the backcourt yet to get back on defense. My brother began to dribble the basketball as soon as he was on the court and dribbled right through those four defenders. He even passed all of us on his team.

He was now on the other side of the court. It was just him and Mr. McDonald's All-American slam dunk champion. Just like a year or so earlier in the varsity match where this guy waited up for a player to dunk over him at the rim, my brother ran down the right side of the court making his way towards another showdown at the rim.

This guy was on the left side and was now running towards the rim to block my brother. This guy was licking his chops to block his shot. This was a McDonald's All-American slam dunk winner and varsity basketball star for Indiana University, playing in front of all these fans. No way was this even going to be a competition.

But my brother was the best player on the court, this guy being no exception. My brother dribbled his way to the right side of the rim. They both jump simultaneously. This guy's hands are well above the rim, almost up towards the top of the box as he slaps the backboard as hard as he could in an attempt to block my brother's layup.

But my brother was better. So much better, that my brother, in mid air as he was going up for the layup, floated in the air with one hand on the basketball, not two as is usual to protect the basketball from being blocked.

My brother was just as cocky and confident as this guy. And that day he proved to be a better showman as well.

As they are both in mid-air and my brother has his right hand going up for the layup, my brother takes his left hand and slaps this guy in the butt mid-air and yells, "Good game!" so that everyone could hear him.

My brother hits the game winning layup over this guy in a showboating fashion that is only respected on the playground courts of America, to not only win the game but to end this guy's career playing basketball on the campus of IU.

After that game, this guy was talking to a lot of the other guys as he gathered up his belongings to leave. He told everyone that he was no longer going to be playing basketball at IU anymore. He was transferring down to the University of Houston where he would become the star.

It proved to be probably the best decision of this guy's career. He went on to star at the University of Houston, becoming one of the nation's leading scorers, and earning a roster spot in the NBA as a backup point guard for both the Utah Jazz and the Indiana Pacers.

Another one of my brother's stories playing basketball at IU was playing against another campus star from the men's basketball team. This guy was a starter for our men's team and was known as one of the best shooters in the country. He had just helped lead our men's team to the national championship game against Maryland in 2002.

My brother was playing with other guys, not his usual squad. This men's basketball player happened to be at the gym that day and ended up playing on the same court as my brother. My brother had to guard this guy, who was a 6 ft 5 sharp shooter. He single handedly shut him down and led his team to victory. He couldn't even get a shot off against my brother.

As for me, I have a few good stories of my own, nothing as big as my brother. One day we played against the best squad I have ever played against. It was a starting five that included a guy who started at the University of Miami Ohio, a guy who started at the University of Wisconsin, that guy's younger brother who started at Syracuse University, and another guy who played for Indiana State University along with a cousin who played Junior College in California.

The guy who played at Miami of Ohio was a friend of ours and we had played against him several times. He was a beast. He was from Indiana originally and played with Pat Knight, Bob Knight's son, in high school. After college, he almost made the Toronto Raptors, being the last person cut, barely beaten out by Cuttino Mobley.

He was a lights out shooter, but only standing 6 ft tall, he was guardable and beatable. But both the brothers stood at 6 ft 6 inches and the guy who played at Indiana State was 6 ft 7. The tallest guy on our squad was maybe 5 ft 10, but he was a beast. He was pound for pound one of the best rebounders on campus. I would put him up against anybody and have confidence in his rebounding ability.

I was guarded by the oldest brother who started at the University of Wisconsin. The younger brother played at Syracuse University where he had just won a national championship in 2003 with Carmelo Anthony. The older brother was guarding me and laid off of me quite a bit.

I hit my first two jump shots without him guarding me. His team mates began to dog him and say that I was killing him. This made him try a bit harder.

The next time I got the ball, I went up for a shot and he jumped out of the gym to block me. Instead of shooting it, I did a pump fake, and just drove around him and went up nice and easy for a layup. My team mates were laughing as well as the rest of his squad.

Now he was starting to pick up his intensity. We ended up closely losing to them 15-13, but not before I went on to score 5 more points on him for a total of 8 points. In a game to 15, that is more than 50% of the points so that was huge. I was balling on a bonafide starter from a Big Ten team.

I was used to guarding bigger guys although I was only 5 ft 8. I was still one of the best rebounders on campus, save for my friend and team mate who was only 5 ft 10 himself. Our squad would usually out-rebound every team. We didn't have to worry about rebounds or getting back on defense. We were quicker, faster and usually stronger than all of our opponents.

The only time I remember getting out rebounded in a game on campus was against a player who was a starting forward for the men's basketball team at IU. He was an absolute beast. He was Mr. Basketball from the state of Georgia and had just helped lead our basketball team to the national championship game. He was a campus favorite as everyone cheered his name during the games. His biggest moment was when he blocked Carlos Boozer at the buzzer to beat Duke University in the sweet 16.

Now, he was on my court playing against our squad. I remember before the game, he told his team out loud so everyone could hear him to not worry about rebounding, that he would grab every rebound. I remember thinking to myself, laughing a little, "He obviously hasn't been on the court with me before."

Every time the ball went up, I was right there going for the rebound. But every time I got my hands on the ball somebody else had their hands on the ball as well. It was this starting forward. What usually were easy rebounds for me, were now being contested by my opponent.

He was 6 ft 4 inches tall and weighed about 225, at least. He looked short on television as he often times had to guard bigger guys 5 or 6 inches taller than him. He still outplayed and outmanned most of his opponents. But here he was, not on television, but standing right next to me. I had the responsibility of blocking him out every shot. I had to overpower him on every possession. It was a tough task.

While he did get several more rebounds than I would have liked, and clearly won the battle between both of us, I got my fair share of rebounds and had consistently battled him on every board. He was just a little stronger than me and had a little more weight on me. I was only 145 lbs at the time and was only benching about 275 lbs at the time. But I knew then, that I was on the level of one of the best rebounders in the country.

I also remember out battling the older brother of another men's basketball player, who was Mr. Basketball from Indiana and started at IU for four years. This guy, who was several years older than his younger brother, had just returned to IU from playing college basketball. He was the same age as me, maybe a year older. I knew him, because I had played against him when I was younger. I hadn't seen him in a while so I didn't recognize him when I walked in the gym that day.

I was by myself and got picked up by a bunch of random guys. Everyone on my squad was afraid to guard him because he was a big player, 6 ft 3 maybe 4 and weighing 230 lbs or so. I was by far the smallest guy on the court, but I always played the biggest and had the biggest heart. I guarded him and we ended up battling the whole game. I ended up winning and I out rebounded him, but I remember at the end of the game asking who he was because I had never played against him or saw him in the gym before. He told me who he was and that he had just transferred back and then it all made sense.

Another time, I remember playing against a men's basketball player who was the eldest son of an IU legend from the 1976 undefeated team and older brother of a player who went on to win a national title with the University of North Carolina and was a lottery pick in the NBA draft. It was the end of his freshman year at IU where he walked on to the men's team. The IU men's team was hoping to recruit his younger brother who was a McDonald's All-American. After his younger brother chose UNC over IU, this guy decided to transfer schools.

But the guy I played against was a point guard, closer to my size. We guarded each other and went head to head, but I dominated, scoring close to 10 of our 15 points and limiting him greatly. Much like my brother beat the slam dunk champion the last time he played at IU before transferring, I beat this guy who was on his way to another school.

But more than just beating guys and battling squads to see who the best was, we just had a lot of fun playing the game we loved.

One of the guys on my intramural team went on to try out for the men's team his senior year at IU. He was good enough to make it and dominated at try outs, but the coaches ended up keeping a younger and taller player, hoping he would develop.

I had a lot of fun and made a lot of friends playing pick-up basketball every day at Indiana University. I then would stick around the game playing pick-up ball here and there but nothing at the level of IU, until I went back just two years ago.

I hadn't played in that HPER gym for almost 10 years, but my brother and I were right back at it. We immediately began winning most of our games and becoming recognized as two of the best players at the gym. Everything was going great until a few weeks into the school year I landed on a player's foot as I jumped up to steal a pass.

Bam. Crack. Shatter. My right ankle was broken and I was laying on the middle of the court. It took over a year for my ankle to fully heal and I decided to hang up my sneakers so that I could walk and enjoy my life.

Life is not fun when you are laying on your bed, unable to walk and having to put your entire foot in a bucket of ice every hour for several months. So I moved down to South Florida for the warm weather and saw immediately how much help people need on their basketball game. I had taken for granted the level of play in Indiana and traveling around the country I have come to find that most players lack the fundamentals of having a good game.

I have played and seen a lot of basketball in my time and that is what has given me the passion to write this e-book. I have been around a lot of players who have played college level basketball and have earned college scholarships because of their skill in the game.

I learned this game and played this game in Indiana. In Indiana, almost every kid knows how to shoot. It's almost like riding a bike.

True story. One of my close friends growing up never played a day of organized basketball in his life. He later went on to serve in the Navy and ended up playing a lot of basketball on the ship. He told me that he was often times the best player on the court and definitely had the best shot. When I played with him, after he returned to his home town to become a recruiter for the Navy, I could tell that he wasn't lying. His shot was almost picture perfect. Yet, he never stood a chance of making any organized team in Indiana.

Another true story. I was traveling through the east coast in the fall and decided to stop at a small college where I had a friend attending. We stopped by the gym and saw the basketball team playing. The coach was really nice and since it was only a pre-season session, he let my brother and I play with them. The team, overall, wasn't the strongest. They had a few guys on the squad who were really good. In fact, one of the best Dwayne Wade step through moves I have ever seen was done by a player on that team, right in front of me. But the best shooter on that team was a guy who never even played organized basketball before. I couldn't believe that he could go directly from not playing basketball ever to playing on a small college team. I then asked him where he was from. Sure enough, he was from small town Indiana just a few miles from where I grew up. It all made sense now.

Next chapter, I will talk more about Indiana basketball, but I want to finish on why I am so passionate about teaching the tools of the shot.

Outside of Indiana, basketball is usually played by athletic players who focus more on speed, strength and athleticism rather than the fundamentals. It really comes down to coaching and having access to this much necessary information. Thankfully, Indiana has a great oral history tradition where this information has been passed down from generation to generation. Learning how to shoot is almost a rite of passage in Indiana.

The shots of many players are not fundamentally sound. Just yesterday I saw a young kid making a shooting motion with his hands in a store. I immediately had to tell him to spread his finger tips. I'm sure nobody has ever told him that in his life. But I had this burning passion to help him out. And so it is with this passion to help coach and train the next generation of great shooters that I write this e-book to add to this illustrious history known as basketball.

In addition, I know that having access to this information is very costly. In order to have access to this type of information, first you have to be lucky enough to find a coach who he himself has been taught the proper techniques. These coaches are usually the better coaches who coach high level basketball teams that cost a lot of money to play on. Even then, when coaches are coaching at a high level, most times their number one priority is to make sure the team wins. This often times does not lead to emphasizing player development and teaching fundamentals. Instead, it focuses on playing the best players, coaching them to their strengths already (which most times includes being fast, strong and athletic) and scouting their opponents to ensure a victory.

The reality is America has a deep, entrenched coaching problem. While there are certainly a hand full of coaches out there who are passionate about the game, like their players and treat them with respect, make sure that players are both having fun and developing as a player as well as being there to instill a few lifelong principles and disburse some nuggets of wisdom along the way, the majority of coaches have either too little knowledge or experience with the game of basketball, care too little about the players and more about their coaching position, care more about winning and less about player development, care more about controlling the players and getting their way then giving the players responsibility and freedom and taking too much credit for victories and placing too much blame on players for losses.

Frankly, many coaches have stolen the joy away from basketball leaving many players receiving none of the benefits yet walking away with all of the negatives the game has to offer.

So that is my rant for the day regarding coaching in America. Coaches: you need to step up. You need to genuinely care about these young men, care about their development as players and people, care more about their improvement than meaningless winning percentages and ensure that these players are having fun and enjoying coming to basketball practice every day. If not, please do these men, basketball and the world a favor, quit!

Obviously, I have experienced my fair share of bad coaching. But thankfully, I have had a few good coaches along the way who actually took a genuine interest in my development and took the time to teach me some fundamentals and gave me the confidence to shoot the ball and play as hard as I can.

But if you don't have access to good coaching or if your coach does not like you, you are pretty much alone in your own development. You are stuck learning from television or from friends.

Another way most players learn how to shoot is by going to basketball camps. Most of these camps are held at a university and become very expensive. I remember most of the guys I played AAU basketball with would go to basketball camps every summer. They would have these amazing stories of having fun in dorms and their game would improve. But they came from very wealthy families and my mom didn't have an extra $500 to send my brother and me away to camp. So we had our driveway or our friend's driveway down the street.

I want to make sure that everyone has access to this information. You don't need to pay thousands of dollars to play on a high level AAU team, you don't need to spend several hundred dollars going to a basketball camp (where you will be just one of several hundred campers anyways) and you don't need to spend a hundred dollars on other books and dvds that frankly just dedicate a page or a few short minutes to the information below.

If you use these tips and tactics, your shot will improve greatly. It will help you make your team. It will possibly help you earn a college scholarship and possibly even give you the opportunity to make a living playing professional basketball in the NBA.

Now, let me share with you some of those greats in the NBA who have grown up with the Indiana basketball tradition.

Chapter 2: The Indiana Basketball Tradition

So, you are wondering why I have put a lot of emphasis on the Hoosier state. Well, not only is it my stomping grounds of where I learned the intricacies of the perfect jump shot, but it is a rare place full of basketball glory. Legends such as UCLA coach John Wooden, the "Big O" Oscar Robertson and even "Larry Legend" himself hail from Indiana. For those of you who don't know who "Larry Legend" is, he is Hall of Famer Larry Bird: NBA champion, Olympic Gold Medalist with the Dream Team, one time rival of Magic Johnson and the current President of the Indiana Pacers.

Other NBA greats have also come out of Indiana as well where they grew up learning the fundamentals and perfecting their game.

We have had several great big men come from the state of Indiana. One of my favorites was Shawn Kemp, the "Reign Man," who electrified the NBA throughout much of the 90's with the Seattle Supersonics. Other notable big men include George McGinnis, 2007 number 1 overall pick Greg Oden, Eric Montross (mostly of UNC fame), NBA all star Brad Miller, lottery picks Jared Jeffries, Zach Randolph and Sean May (all of whom I played against while growing up), and recent big men, brothers Tyler and Cody Zeller and Miles and Mason Plumlee.

Indiana also has its fair share of great point guards. These guards are highly recognizable and well respected in the NBA today. Guys such as starters Mike Conley, Jr. with the Memphis Grizzlies and Jeff Teague currently with the Indiana Pacers battled it out in central Indiana as they were growing in their game.

Indiana has had some great scorers and shooters as well. Glenn Robinson was drafted number one overall in the NBA ahead of guys like Jason Kidd and Grant Hill and landed the largest rookie contract in NBA history. Indiana also adds Calbert Cheaney to its list of amazing scorers, the Indiana University great who set the collegiate scoring record for the Big Ten Conference. Both of these players had amazing jump shots. These players paved the way for other Indiana shooters in the NBA such as Eric Gordon, Gordon Hayward, and Gary Harris.

And that's not even mentioning all the other great college players from Indiana. A quick shout out to guys like Damon Bailey (Indiana University), Bryce Drew (Valparaiso), Jason Gardner (University of Arizona), Chris Thomas (University of Notre Dame), Luke Harangody (University of Notre Dame), and Deshaun Thomas (Ohio State University).

But even greater than all these players that Indiana has developed, it has been the amazing minds of basketball that have come out of the Hoosier state that has truly revolutionized the sport. So many great coaches at every level have roots in Indiana. Current college coaches such as Steve Alford (UCLA), Calbert Cheaney (St. Louis University), and Matt Painter (Purdue University) have all benefitted from their time in Indiana playing basketball. NBA head coaches such as Scott Skiles (Orlando Magic), Brad Stevens (Boston Celtics), Randy Whitman (Washington Wizards), and Mike Woodson (New York Knicks) have an Indiana pedigree.

And arguably the greatest coach of all time, with the possible exceptions of John Wooden, Red Auerbach and Phil Jackson, is Gregg Popovich of the NBA's San Antonio Spurs. You guessed it. He too is from Indiana. For those of you who haven't watched an

NBA game the last 15 years, he is the mastermind of the big three of Duncan, Parker and Ginobili who has sustained success during three different eras of the NBA.

So basketball is definitely in the water in Indiana, maybe even in the blood!

Chapter 3: The Dominance of Stephen Curry

Stephen Curry's basketball career has not turned out the way many expected. In fact, it has not turned out the way anyone expected. Except for maybe Stephen Curry's mother, who is his biggest supporter and can always be seen courtside wearing his apparel and cheering for his every move.

Stephen in many ways was like many other young basketball players growing up: undersized and overlooked. But Stephen had one huge advantage that 99 percent of basketball players never have. He had a dad who was a professional NBA basketball player.

Growing up, Stephen was able to travel with his dad to his games. Stephen was able to attend his practices, shoot around with his teammates, hang out in the locker rooms and just be around the NBA game. If anyone had an advantage to make it to the NBA it was Stephen.

His dad Dell Curry, at the time, was one of the best pure shooters in the game. Dale was known for his shooting and scoring ability, especially when it came to knocking down three's. Although he was not the most athletic or talented guy in the NBA during the era of Jordan, he was one the most skilled spot up shooters of his era. Dell finished his career as the all-time leading scorer in Charlotte Hornets history.

While Stephen had been around the NBA game ever since he was born, not many thought of him as NBA prospect. In fact, only one school heavily recruited him with a Division 1 scholarship offer. As a senior, he was barely 6-0 tall and only weighed a rail-thin 160 pounds. One commenter said that Stephen looked like he was 14 years old as a senior in high school.

It turned out, going to Davidson College was one of the best things that could have ever happened to Stephen Curry.

Instead of being discouraged by the lack of interest from ACC schools, Curry began immediately showing the country, and his doubters, his skill and talent. He scored 32 points against Michigan in his second career college game and led his team to a NCAA tournament berth with a 29-5 season record.

He then led Davidson on a 19-0 winning record and one shot short of reaching the Final Four. Although he entertained ideas of entering into the NBA draft, he came back for his junior year to prove to everyone that he could play point guard. His sophomore year he was just running off screens and had an amazing point guard and offense that set him up for all his shots and all his points. Now he not only had the ball in his hands but was a target for every opponent's defense.

Despite getting all the attention night in and night out from his opponents, Stephen led the league in scoring that year at 28.6 points per game.

I knew when I saw him during his sophomore year playing, that he had incredible skill. I knew that he was more than just a shooter. I knew that he was more than just a scorer. I knew that he was an incredible talent that had unbelievable court vision, awareness and passing abilities. Unfortunately, many of his teammates were not on the same elite level as him. That is why I knew he would be a star once he entered the NBA.

I thought that Stephen Curry should have been the number one overall pick in the 2009 NBA draft. Yet instead, he was overlooked once again and fell to a club that was considered one of the worst in the NBA at the time: the Golden State Warriors. Although Curry had a strong rookie showing, averaging 17.5 points a game, almost 6 assists and 2 steals a game and finishing second in

Rookie of the Year voting, his next few seasons were plagued with reoccurring ankle injuries.

Due to his injuries many in the sports world wrote off Stephen. It was considered a risky move by Golden State Warriors to resign Stephen given his injury problems. But Stephen, just like he did in high school and just like he did in college, when he was overlooked and written off, came back with a vengeance.

Stephen Curry became one of the most exciting players in all of the NBA. He became one of the most prolific scorers in NBA history and solidified his rank as the greatest shooter in NBA history by breaking the 3 point single season record three years in a row. Curry took it to a whole other level when he led his team to an NBA title and won the league's MVP award during the 2014-2015 season.

When everyone thought he had reached his peak and maxed out his talent, Stephen Curry proved everyone wrong again when he shattered his own three point record, became the first person in NBA history to win the league MVP unanimously and led his team to a league record 73-9.

Just when you thought it could not get any better, Stephen Curry starts off the 2016-2017 season by breaking the single game record for three pointers made in a game. Curry hit 13 3-Pointers against the New Orleans Pelicans.

Stephen Curry is the most exciting player in the NBA. He may arguably be the most exciting player to ever play the game. In today's game when guard play dominates the league, Stephen Curry and the Golden State Warriors' brand of unselfish basketball that relies heavily on cutting, passing and shooting is the Gold Standard for basketball today.

Chapter 4: The Importance of the Jump Shot

The jump shot is important because it is a way to put points on the board. It is sometimes the easiest shot in the game to get off, while at the same time being one of the hardest shots to make.

Think about it. If you can dunk, that is a higher percentage shot. If you can drive past your defender and make a layup, that is a higher percentage shot. But in reality, while those shots are higher percentage and often times considered much easier shots, I believe those shots have a higher degree of difficulty. Not in the shot themselves, but in the circumstances surrounding them.

In order to get a dunk, often times you have to run, dribble, jump and make a shot. Same thing goes with a layup. But many times, especially at higher levels, you have to dribble past players, you have to drive in traffic, you have to sustain contact and you have to go against more than one defender. You will have guys who are 7 feet tall jumping at you, stronger guys hacking at you and faster guys getting in your way to stop you.

Think about it. You are watching an NBA game and towards the end LeBron James has the ball. All of a sudden instead of driving to the basket and getting a dunk or layup like he has being doing earlier in the game, he decides to take a jump shot from the top of key. Why? Because he is tired of driving all game and having to take on the entire rest of the team. It is much easier to shoot a 20 foot jump shot with limited defense. It just makes sense. A jump shot is the easiest shot to take, but the hardest to make.

That is why becoming an amazing jump shooter is your ticket to earn a college scholarship!

You don't have to be the tallest player. You don't have to be the fastest player. You don't have to be the best dribbler or passer. If you have a great, fundamental jump shot you can earn a scholarship and make a team. You will find a way to earn court time. You can even find yourself on an NBA roster making millions.

True story. A guy from my high school was a horrible basketball player in the general sense. He was slow, he was not athletic, and he didn't have much heart, passion or intensity. He wasn't tall nor did he make his team mates better. Overall, he deserved to be in the middle of the cheering section more than he did to wear a basketball uniform. Yet, the one thing he could do was shoot the basketball, if he ever got open. He would literally, every play, run to the corner and just sit there waiting for the ball. If he caught it, he would try to get a shot off and most likely it had a decent chance of going in. He was not a varsity level athlete in basketball, but he earned a varsity letter strictly because of his jump shot.

So grab out your basketball and start putting these tips into practice. Soon enough you will be getting attention from coaches and will stand out with your perfect jump shot!

Chapter 5: Lower Body Mechanics

The jump shot begins and ends with your feet. That's why we are going to start off looking at your lower body when perfecting your shot. Remember, that your legs are what power your shot, not your arms.

There are 5 things you must do with your lower body to ensure you have a perfect shot.

Square your feet to the basket.

What this means is that you should get yourself into a shooting position before you receive the ball. Your feet, or at least one foot, should be firmly planted, facing the basket when you catch the ball. You can always tell which way the ball will go if you only look at the shooters feet. If the feet are pointing to the right, the shot will go to the right. So make sure that your feet are facing the basket when you shoot. Keep them facing the basket throughout the entire shooting process from beginning to end.

True Story. My brother became an amazing shooter. He was so good that almost every shot he took you could bet it was going in. Well recently, his shot has been off. I began looking at his shot and trying to coach him to get back to where his shot was. I was only looking at his upper body. I thought that he was shooting the ball outside of his shooting pocket closer to his head, I thought he was pushing the ball more than releasing it, I thought a few other things as well.

After correcting those issues, his shot was still off. It was not until I looked at the lower half of his body that I recognized the biggest culprit. It was his feet. His feet were actually pointed to the right, towards the corner of the court, rather than directly straight towards the basket. He couldn't correct his feet, because it turns out that he has slight scoliosis now where his back is all twisted, his hips are off and his feet naturally turn towards the side. He won't be able to fix his shot until he fixes his back. But regardless of how good of a shooter he is, without his feet being able to be straight and facing towards the basket, his percentage will stay low.

Get your legs under you.

What that means is that after you square your feet to the basket you need to be sure that your legs are in line with your body and ready to load. If your legs are leaning towards a certain direction or taking your body forward you will not be able to stay set for the shooting motion and it will affect your shot. Make sure you have your legs directly under your shoulders, shoulder width apart, ready to jump straight, not sideways.

Bend your knees.

When you shoot a shot, whether it is a jump shot or a set shot such as a free throw, make sure that you bend your knees. This is often times the number one reason why a player shoots the ball short. The more you bend your knees, the more power you will get when you jump, allowing your shot to go further. Make sure you don't bend too much or too slow. This will allow defenders to defend your shot a lot easier. Practice bending your knees and using your legs to power up your shot.

True Story. Before I learned more about shooting, I only focused on the upper half of my body. I had a decent looking shot, but I was always short and my percentage was low. Thankfully, I had a coach who told me to bend my knees and that my strength should actually come from my legs. After making this adjustment, I then was able to get the ball to the rim every time and my shot both looked and felt better.

Make sure your waist is also square to the basket.

This is very important. Your waist is what joins your lower body to your upper body. If your feet are squared to the basket, but your waist is shifting to the right, it will make your shot go right. Make sure that your waist is aligned with your feet and legs, squarely facing the basket in front of you. Your waist will dictate where your torso and shoulders will be facing.

Jump forward towards the basket

Most players when they start off will just jump straight up and down. This is much better than jumping side to side, but it is not what you want to do if you are trying to perfect your shot. You want to square your feet, lock and load your legs, bend your knees and with a straight waist jump up and slightly forward towards the basket on your shot.

You don't want to overdo it, but just jump forward slightly. If you start your shot behind the three point line, you should land either on the line or in front of the line depending on your comfort level. This will help you reach the basket more on your longer shots and keep you from shooting the ball short.

Chapter 6: Upper Body Mechanics

Now we will discuss the mechanics of your shot using your upper body. There are so many parts of the shot that must come together for the ball to go in. Below are the proper mechanics to have a perfect shot. I will mostly be describing a right handed shot, since most shooters are right handed. If you are left handed you can do the same things, yet just switch right and left hands/arms.

Catch the ball in your shooting pocket

What this means is that I often see so many shooters who start out their shooting motion with the ball all over the place. The ball could be down at their hips (which makes it a lot easier for a defender, especially one shorter than you, to be able to block the shot). The ball could be on the opposite side of the body from their shooting hand (which will not allow a fluid up and down shooting motion). They could catch it at head level or even above their head.

You want to be sure to catch the ball in your shooting pocket. If you are a right handed shooter, you will catch it around your right chest and shoulder area above your stomach. If you are a left handed shooter, you will catch it around your left chest and shoulder area above your stomach.

Most coaches will teach that you should catch the ball in a triple threat position. Your shooting pocket is the triple threat position. You can, depending on which way your elbow points (up for a shot, out and backwards for a pass and down for a dribble) shoot, pass and dribble out of this position. That is why it is called a triple threat.

This is important because as you move up in levels of play, you want to be able to have multi facets to your game so that your shot will not be as predictable. If you just focus on catching the ball and starting with the ball in your shooting pocket (or triple threat position) your accuracy will go up. Where you catch the ball is the most important first mechanic in the upper body because it will set up the rest of your shot.

True Story. One of my best friends growing up had me help him work on his jump shot. He was determined to have the best shot in the country, if not all time. That was just the person he was. He was training for the NBA at the time. So I watched him take a few shots and realized he had a lot wrong with his mechanics.

He grew up playing power forward and was a rebounding machine. He only grew to be 6 ft 3 inches. And although he still was very strong and skilled as a big man, he had to adjust his game and develop guard skills in order to make it to the highest level. So to say that his shot was raw was an understatement.

Immediately, I saw that he was catching the ball and starting his shooting motion from his lower left hip area. He was a right handed shooter but by starting at his bottom left hip area, he had to bring the ball all the way across his body and then go up for the shot.

This did three things. First, he didn't quite have control of the ball because he would catch it and place it by his left hip, then the whole time as he was bringing it across his body he would try to get a good grip on it. The shot was doomed for failure from the beginning.

Second, because he was bringing the ball across his body instead of starting with it in his shooting pocket, his overall stroke was not fluid and it was not a straight up and down motion like it should have been. Instead, it was sort of this funky left to right, then back to the left sort of motion that left his elbow way out and pointing to the side.

And third, because he started with the ball so low on his hip and took so much time to gain control and bring it back over to his shooting side, it was much easier for a player, especially a taller player, to have the time to block it.

So I worked with him getting comfortable catching the ball in his right side shooting pocket and not dropping the ball down to his left hip. This made his overall shot a lot better and faster and led to a greater looking shot and one with a lot more accuracy.

You want to be set in your shooting motion when you catch the ball

What this means is that if you are a jump shooter and you want to shoot the ball when you catch it, you must be set in your shooting motion ready for the ball when it is passed to you. So make sure your feet are set, squared to the basket. Make sure your legs are bent at the knees ready to explode when you receive the ball. And most importantly, make sure that your hands are in the shooting motion, waiting at the shooting pocket as you call for the ball.

Place your right hand out about six inches from your shooting shoulder in a natural, normal position you would if you had the ball in your hand. Place your left hand just to the side of it as if you have a basketball already in your hand. This lets your team mates know that you are ready to shoot the ball and it also lets you have your two hands ready to catch the pass. In addition, it is beneficial at times to jump into the pass as you catch it to set up your shooting motion.

Get your hands in the shooting position

You want to catch the ball with your hands in shooting position. Your right hand should be in the middle of the ball and your left hand should be at the left side of the ball. Your left hand is there simply to assist your right hand in balancing the ball and making sure that it does not slide away. It is merely a guide hand and should not be used to shoot the ball in the air.

Seam the basketball

When you watch some of the best shooters you can see their rotation on the ball and it looks so beautiful. The reason it looks so pretty is because they have spent lots of practice time getting their hands on the right spot of the ball so that their rotation will look flawless.

To seam the ball, however the ball is when you catch it, make sure you rotate it so that your fingers are perpendicular to the lines going across the ball. What this means is that your finger tips should not be parallel to the black seams. So that when you shoot the ball in the air, your rotation will reveal a perfect rotation of black seams.

You must continually practice seaming the ball when you catch it every time. You will get better grip, better feeling and a better looking shot. After a while, you will not even notice that you are consciously rotating the ball in your hands before you shoot. It will become second nature.

For more advanced shooters who are playing against faster and longer defenders, you may need to work on shooting the ball against the seams, simply because you can't afford the extra second or half second it takes to seam the ball. Then you can practice shooting against the seam and getting used to the ball in your hands in different ways. But this is only for shooters who have mastered shooting the proper way with the seams.

Place your shooting hand in the middle of the ball

This is important because if your hand is not squarely in the middle of the ball, your shot will be off. It will float either to the left or the right depending on which side of the ball your dominant shooting hand is. You want it to be directly in the middle of the ball for balance and control.

Setting up the T

This is possibly the most important part of your shooting motion when it comes to your hands. If you properly set up the T shape with your hands on the ball, both your hands will be in proper position to shoot the ball accurately. To establish a T, look at both of your thumbs on the ball. Your right hand should be in the middle of the ball with your thumb facing up and to the right (right handed shooters).

Your left hand should be at the side of the ball with your left thumb just a half inch or so slightly above your right thumb making the top part of the t, or a perpendicular line above the right thumb.

This T shape with your thumbs ensures that your hands are in the correct positions: your right hand in the middle under the ball and your left hand on the side ready to assist. Look for the T shape every time you shoot the ball when starting on your new shot. After a while, you will get used to the positioning of your hands on the ball and you won't have to think about it.

So you will only use your right hand in the actual shot. Your left hand is only to be a guide and will not be involved in the releasing of the ball. This is very important. You want a one handed jumper like the pros, not a two handed jumper like my friend Jordan.

True Story. In college, I had a friend by the name of Jordan. He grew up in Santa Monica, in the LA area. He was an avid basketball fan and all-out hooper. He picked Indiana University just because of its culture of pickup basketball on campus. Our campus has a gym called the HPER (today it is the Wildermuth Intramural Center) that has a huge field house with 10 courts. Every day of the week, any time from 3pm until Midnight when it closes, you can find at least 10 guys in there playing a pickup basketball game. At times, every court is full and there are several hundred guys in the gym at the same time playing. It is truly a sight to see.

Well, back to my buddy Jordan. We were playing together one day at the HPER and we happened to play against some of the players from our school's football team. We were obviously better, but the other team had this one football player. He was our school's star running back and wide receiver. He stood almost 6 ft 4 inches and just recently set our school record for most touchdowns in a game, 6.

Although this guy chose to play football in college, he was an outstanding basketball player in high school, almost earning our state's top honor of Mr. Basketball. He could have played almost anywhere he wanted in basketball as well.

On the court, he was a one man show, but we had a team. And that day our team was led by my friend Jordan. He was on fire. He was hitting all of his shots.

Then all of a sudden, the running back started yelling out "Two Scoops" every time my buddy Jordan would shoot the ball.

He was confused and was like, "What the heck? Why does he keep yelling that when I shoot it?"

We were laughing and had to break it to him that although he was a good player (mostly just a scrappy guy who played defense and outran guys for layups) he shot the ball using both hands. It looked like a two scoop shot. He was a little late in his playing career and only played for fun, so he didn't work on perfecting his shot. But it was funny how players will immediately notice your two handed shot, even if it is going in.

Another True Story. My brother used to shoot like Reggie Miller. Although I love and respect him, he is a hero to almost every

Hoosier who grew up or lived in the state from 1987 until 2007, I do not recommend you emulate his shot. He would use his left thumb in this shot and would look like he shot the ball with two hands.

Well, my brother used to shoot like this until my AAU coach in practice one day taped his left thumb to his left index finger. This disallowed him from using his off-hand thumb in his shot. He then had to get used to stroking the ball with just his right hand and only using his left hand as a guide.

You may have to use this tip as well if you find that your off-hand thumb continues to get in the way of your shot.

Setting up the V (Using Your Fingertips)

A simple way to remember the proper way to set up your hands for a perfect shot is to think about TV. The T shape is formed with your thumbs, which we discussed in number 6. The V shape is going to be formed with your shooting palm. It is a slight V, but a V nonetheless.

Most shooters make the mistake of resting the ball on the palm of their shooting hand. This is a big no no. You want the ball to rest on the pads of your fingertips, not your palm. You also want to make sure that you actually spread your fingertips.

This will allow much better grip with the ball leading to more control and accuracy in your shot. When the ball is on the fingertips of your hand, this will automatically form a V with your shooting hand palm. Make sure the V is there. Practice making this shape. It will then become second nature.

Elbow In

Most of the shooters I work with make the natural mistake of keeping their elbow out to their side when they shoot. It looks like a chicken wing. This will greatly affect your shot in a negative way. Instead, you want to make sure that your elbow is in towards your side and directly above your right knee. Where your elbow begins in your shot will determine how fluid your shooting motion will be. Start with your elbow in, above your knee, ready to explode straight up past your shoulder and into your release.

L shape Elbow

When you go up for your shot, your elbow should be in an L shape above your shoulder. In fact, if you want to perfect this motion, you should look like you are a waiter in a fancy restaurant. Your shoulder should be in an L shape, with your wrist closer to your head bent backwards like you are carrying a heavy tray of food out to people in a restaurant. If you do this position right, it will ensure that you are not pushing the ball but rather shooting it with control and accuracy. It will also make it harder for a defender to block your shot.

Elbow Straight during the shot

The next most common mistake of shooters I work with is that their elbow does not stay straight throughout the shooting motion. You want to start with your elbow in and above your knee. You want to go straight up through your shot. Then you want to make sure that your elbow remains straight during your follow through motion.

Shoulders

Make sure that your shoulders are square to the basket. If your shoulders are facing a different direction your shot will be ineffective. Wherever your shoulders are facing, that is where the ball will end up. Make sure your shoulders are relaxed and facing the basket.

Release

    This is a point of much contention in the shooting community. Most of us agree that you should be releasing the ball on the way up rather than at the end of your shot. This will ensure that the ball has enough power behind it to get to the basket. If you release the ball at the end of your shot when your elbow is fully extended, it will not have any power. If you release it too early, you will be shooting from a lower position, making it harder for the ball to get to the basket and easier for it to be blocked. You want to be sure to release it smoothly in the motion of your upward shot.

Rotation/Back spin/Wrist

Your shot will essentially be the ball coming off the flick of your fingertips. Your wrist will snap forward and create and sort of an upside down C in the air. Some call it a parachute.

You want to flick your wrist when you release the ball to create a great backspin rotation. This will make the ball softer if it hits the rim and will give it a better chance of going in.

When you flick your wrist and release the ball, make sure that it is your middle finger that creates the most power on your shot. Your middle finger should be pointing downward and your hand should look like a swan. Your middle finger should look like it is going over the rim and landing inside of it. If your other fingers are more prominent in the shot your shot will usually go slightly right or left.

You can usually tell how good a shot is by looking at the rotation of the ball and the backspin. If it looks pretty, then it has a higher chance of going in. If it looks funky and all over the place then most likely it won't go in.

Arc

Make sure that your shot has a high arc on it. Not too high, but you definitely don't want to shoot a line drive at the basket. If your shot has a nice arc, then it has a better chance of going through the hoop as the rim becomes bigger the higher you shoot it. You also have a better shot at swishing the ball through the net. The lower the arc, the more likely it will hit the rim and bounce out.

You want to shoot for your ball to arc as high as the top of the backboard. If your shot is going much higher than the backboard, that is too much. If it is not going much higher than the square on the backboard, that is not enough. Your arc will determine the percentage of your shots made.

True Story. In elementary school, my shot used to have a very high arc on it. It was so noticeable that my AAU coach that season tried to give me the nickname "Archie." My shot was consistently going higher than the backboard, even on my free throws. Although I made a lot of shots, I worked hard on getting my shot to have a normal arc that was not so unusual.

Follow Through:

    The follow through, some argue, is possibly the most important factor in determining if your shot will go in or not. Most times, coaches and fans can look at a shooter's follow through and know exactly whether the shot is going in or out. You want to be sure to have a great follow through and have your coaches and fans expecting your shot to go in every time.

    In order to have a perfect follow through, you must keep your elbow straight in the air. Keep your wrist snapped as if you are reaching out over the rim. You want to keep your left guide hand also in the air next to your shooting hand. You want to keep it up in the air for at least a second or two after the shot. If you are shooting a free throw, you keep it up until the ball goes in or hits the rim. If you are shooting in a half court set, keep it up long enough to give the shot a chance at going in.

Even if the ball has already left your hands, if your follow through is not straight, it can affect your shot. So keep your follow through straight and hold it in the air.

Head

Make sure your head is straight towards the basket. Not looking up, not looking down, and not looking to the side. If your head is straight and not bobbing up and down, it will keep your balance straight and give you a better looking and more consistent shot.

Eyes

Your eyes determine where you focus your attention. They determine where you are shooting the ball. They determine where your ball will end up. To understand the importance of your eyes, try closing them and then shooting the ball. How well can you shoot now? Not very good, I bet. So you want to be sure that your eyes are focused on the shot.

You want to focus your eyes on the center of the rim, in the middle. As a shooter, I often times focus on the back on the rim because I consistently shoot the ball short. You do not, however, want to focus on the front of the rim. This will always guarantee that your shot will be short and you will miss 100 percent of those shots.

Whatever you do, do not look at the ball while it is in flight. Keep your focus on the goal.

True Story. My brother used to have a funky shot. He actually used to shoot the ball right in front of his face. He did this because, he didn't know it at the time, but he was left eye dominant.

What this means is that he sees everything through his left eye. The majority, 75 percent, of people are right eye dominant. Therefore, it is easier for them to shoot from their right side pocket. The rest, 25 percent, are left eye dominant. Most coaches and players don't know how to catch this.

Once he figured out that he was left eye dominant, he would line his left leg to the center of the basket, not his right leg, like most of us were taught. He then was able to shoot the ball from his right shoulder area and his percentage went way up.

But depending on what eye is dominant for you, you want to line up to the basket using that eye. For instance, if you are right eye dominant, make sure that the right side of your body, your right foot, leg and shoulder is squarely looking towards the center of the basket. If you are left eye dominant, make sure that the entire left side of your body is facing the basket.

The best way to determine what eye dominance you have is to take your hand and make a circle. Focus on an object far away from you across the room. Make sure that you look through the circle and see the object. Then keep that object in the circle and bring your hand closer to your eyes. Whichever eye keeps that object in focus when you get closer to your eyes is your dominant eye. Bring the circle to both your left and your right eye to be sure.

Another test is to take your thumb and cover up an object across the room. Then close each eye. Whichever eye continues to see your thumb cover up the object is your dominant eye.

Chapter 7: The Stephen Curry Jump Shot

The fundamentals of the jump shot is the foundation for any good basketball player. The mechanics that were discussed in the previous chapters are the basis for the jump shots for many of the greatest shooters of all time. You can see all of these mechanics in shooters like Larry Bird, Ray Allen and today with Klay Thompson. All of these guys are considered among the greatest basketball shooters ever.

But when it comes to the NBA and shooting over guys who are longer, taller, faster and more athletic than any other league in the world, guys like Stephen Curry who are considered undersized has had to make a few slight adjustments to his shooting motion in order to be more effective as a scorer.

Stephen Curry grew up under the tutelage of his dad Dell Curry who had a more traditional jump shot, like the one kids are taught every day in basketball gyms across the state of Indiana. Yet, he had the intelligence to cater his specific jump shot to the pace, speed and athleticism of the current game.

Let's break down some of the finer mechanics of Stephen Curry's jump shot.

First off, Curry has a great motion that uses both his lower body and upper body in unison to form a beautiful stroke. Curry is less of a spot-up shooter and more of a fluid shooter who can shoot both off the dribble and off the ball.

Stephen Curry keeps his shooting shoulder, his elbow and his right hip aligned. He positions the ball just above his right eye, which is his shooting eye, just before he goes into his shooting motion.

Stephen delineates slightly from the fundamentals of the shooting motion in both his lower body and upper body mechanics.

With his lower body, Stephen actually prefers to not face his feet directly towards the rim. Instead, he lines his feet just slightly left of the rim so that his right side of his body can be closer and more aligned with the basket. When Stephen is shooting off of the dribble, he will jump with his feet square to the basket, but in mid-air will shift his body to the left to align the right side of his body with the basket.

Curry is a wide stance shooter who places his feet a little further out than shoulder width. He then bends his knees in towards each other as he then launches into his jump shot. This gives him increased balance, coordination and power to lift off as he shoots long range jumpers. This also helps him get off of the ground quicker as he often times has a taller, longer defender quickly approaching.

While Curry perfectly sets up into shooting motion with his hands ready and his knees bent, instead of keeping the ball at chest level, he dips the ball below his waist to get the ball into his shooting pocket. This is his shooting motion that he has perfected. This gets him in rhythm as he is able to get a feel for the ball the entire time he dips the ball and brings it up to his right eye.

Normally this is not taught as there are usually many negative consequences from dipping the ball. First, the more you dip the ball, the longer you have the ball in your hands. This gives your defenders more time to react and block you shot. In addition, when you start your shooting motion below your waist this also allows shorter defenders to reach in and block your shot. Not to mention the more steps you have in your shooting motion the more opportunities you have to have poor shooting mechanics.

But Stephen has figured out a way to get in motion and quickly release the ball. The reason he has perfected this is because he gets low and is already set up with his lower body ready for the jump shot. Most times when he is shooting off of the dribble, he is already low and the ball is already at his hip, so he does not have to dip.

Stephen's upper body mechanics slightly differ from the mechanics taught in this book. First off, instead of shooting with the ball directly on his fingertips, he starts the ball on his palm. This may be because most shooters are comfortable with the ball on their palm. Plus shooters with smaller hands may need to use their palm to get a grip on the ball. Although, Stephen starts with the ball on his palm, he finishes his shot by making sure that the ball is flicked by fingertips at the point of release. His middle finger touches the ball last as his wrist then snaps downward creating his beautiful rotation.

He starts his shooting hand just a little to the right of the ball instead of directly underneath. But as he goes up into his shooting motion, he gets his palm and hand directly under the ball. Then he tucks in his left thumb as he releases the ball and his off-hand points a little forward towards the basket as opposed to staying still.

At the set point, Stephen has a 90 degree angle with his upper arm and his torso at his armpit. He has a 45 degree angle with his upper arm and his forearm as the ball is positioned just above his right eye. He reaches his set point as his knees are bent and he is about to jump. Then when his feet leave the ground he releases the ball when he is at his highest point. He uses the power of his jump to push the ball forward towards the rim.

On the release, Curry keeps his wrist loose and floppy as well as his elbow straight. Stephen keeps his eyes on the rim when he shoots, but then immediately puts them on the ball as he watches it rotate through the air.

Curry has spent years and years perfecting his shot and getting comfortable with it. That is the key to being a good shooter. Consistency. Make sure that you follow the fundamentals, mechanics and guidelines written above. But most importantly, make sure that your body feels comfortable and you feel confident in your shot. If you do this with the fundamentals in mind, you will be a better shooter than Stephen Curry.

Chapter 8: Mindset

As a shooter, you have to have a shooter's mindset. This means having a positive attitude at all times. If you miss a shot, believe that you will make the next one. Always believe that every shot you shoot is going in. You have to be mentally tough when it comes to becoming a great shooter.

One way to begin believing that you will make every shot is visualization. Visualize your shot going in. Visualize during warm ups, during practice, while you are laying in bed at night, in the morning when you wake up, and right before you release the ball.

Confidence plays a big part in a shooter's mindset. I'm sure you have seen guys who do not have a great stroke, but because they have confidence, their shot goes in a lot. When they have confidence in themselves, their coach also has confidence in them.

Also, you can see a guy with a great stroke, but who is lacking confidence, and his shot will often miss. You can have the right mechanics, but if you have the wrong mindset your shot will not go in. You could have the worst mechanics, but the right mindset, and you will shoot a higher percentage.

If you couple the right mechanics with a great mindset, then you will have a jump shot that will be as beautiful and deadly as Stephen Curry!

Chapter 9: Last Tips

Perfect practice makes perfect

Be sure to practice all these techniques together perfectly. Perfect practice will make your shot perfect.

Use some drills to get better

Lay on your bed at night or on the floor of your living room and practice shooting and releasing the ball. Make sure the ball is on your finger tips with your left hand as a guide forming a T. Make sure that the ball is resting on your spread fingertips, you are seaming the ball and snapping your wrist to create a perfect backspin rotation.

Another drill is to start shooting the ball using your new form close to the basket then work your way out. You never want to start warming up before a game shooting long shots. You want to start with layups, then 5 feet, then 10 feet, then free throws, then eventually make it out to the three point line. You can tell who is a good shooter by the way they warm up. So start up close!

Play a game called "All around the World."

True Story. Most kids grow up playing HORSE, but I had the fortune of learning about the game "All around the World." This is how I became a great shooter from all over the court. I actually learned about this game from my best friend in first grade whose dad taught us. He would shoot with us from time to time, then we would emulate his shot and the game.

You start on the left block. Then you have two shots to make that shot to move to the next shot. You then go from each hash mark on the free throw line around it and back. If you miss your second shot you have to return to the beginning. This drill/game will get you better and more comfortable shooting from all over the court.

Another drill is to work on catching and shooting with a partner passing you the ball. Make sure you get set on your shot and get into shooting position when you catch the ball.

Advanced shooters can practice with the passer charging them and putting a hand up in their face to block the shot or distract the shooter. This will help you with developing a quicker release and practicing more in-game situations.

Warm Up

Make sure you warm up before each game. Every player is different. Some players need to warm up for a long period of time to get comfortable with their shot and get into a rhythm. Other players, like myself, the more they shoot the worst their shot becomes. So if that is your case, you don't want to warm up excessively. You want to save your shots for the game.

Find Your Range

This is important. Regardless of how much you practice and how well you shoot, every player will have their own specific range. Find out which spots on the court you are best at and focus your efforts on getting to those spots and hitting shots from there. Your team mates will eventually learn where you like to shoot from and will start to look for you there.

True Story. For me, no matter how much I practice, no matter how much I lift weights, no matter how much I mentally prepare, the three point line is just simply out of my range. I am the king at the mid range shot, especially just inside key.

I can consistently knock down 15-17 foot jumpers all day long, but once I take just one step back across the three point line, my shot is off and my percentage goes way down. So I know to stay in my range and take most of my shots from that area.

My other good friend who has played a lot longer than me, loves the corner shots. That is his spot. That is his range. Therefore, when we play, he always runs to the corner. If he ever receives the ball there, regardless of how great of defense is played on him, if he shoots the ball it is most likely going in.

Find your range and stick to it. If you are serious about becoming a three point shooter then simply work on your lower body to increase your range. But smart, effective players play within themselves and within their range.

Free Throw

On your free throw make sure that your body is correctly lined up to the basket. If you are right eye dominant, make sure that your right foot and leg is in the center of the basket. You can tell where your foot should go on indoor courts because most good courts will have a small, little hole in the middle of the free throw line. This signifies the middle of the basket. Place your right foot there if you are right eye dominant and your left foot directly in front of the circle if you are left eye dominant.

You want to make sure that you have a routine that you use and follow on every free throw. Most of the times you want to incorporate a few dribbles in your free throw. My brother and I, and many guys, would usually dribble three times.

You can also do a little back spin rotation to get a better feel and grip on the ball before you shoot it. This pre-shot routine will help you get relaxed, make you comfortable and give you a better feel for the ball when shooting a high pressured shot.

Make sure you bend your knees and don't leave your feet. You will not shoot a jump shot on a free throw. Hold your follow through until the ball hits the rim or goes through the net. Make sure that your eyes focus on the center of the rim the entire time.

Free throws are hard sometimes because you are not being guarded, it is not in the flow of the offense and you are the center of attention. Do what you must to block out unruly fans who are trying to distract you and other thoughts that may be going on in your head.

Visualize the ball going in and have supreme confidence in your shot. Make sure you practice shooting free throws a lot. This is a good warm up before practice or a good drill after practice.

Bank Shot

When shooting a bank shot, use the same technique, but focus your eyes and aim at the top corner of the square on the backboard if you are shooting from the side or the top of the square if you are shooting straight out from the basket.

Using Screens to get open for a Shot

Practice getting open by properly using a screen. Make sure you set up your man by using a V cut, then rubbing your defender off of the screener once the screener is set. You can practice rounding the screener and rolling towards the basket or you can flair away from the basket separating from the defender and creating space for your shot.

Shooting off the dribble

Work on shooting off the dribble. Work on the stop and pop. This is a different motion, but allow your dribble to get your body set and in a shooting motion. You want to be able to bring the ball directly up off the dribble into your shooting pocket and continue on with the rest of the mechanics. Practice this.

3 Pointers and Long shots

Make sure you really use your legs here on these long shots. It is all about the legs. Don't try to use more shoulder, arms or wrist action in your shot. It will throw your shot off and your percentage will go down. Instead, try jumping higher and landing closer to the basket. You can also do a little less arc here than a closer shot so that it will not be short.

Wear proper shoes

You want to wear a nice pair of indoor basketball shoes if you can. Most importantly you want to wear a pair of shoes that fit you. I know in the basketball community there is a misconception, especially among younger players, that the size of shoes you wear can mean how good of a player you are. It doesn't. If your feet are a size 10, wear a size 10. Don't try to act bad and put on a size 12 so you can brag to your friends. That will only lead to horrible game and possibly injuries.

Chapter 10: Closing Thoughts

Anyone can become a great shooter. Any great shooter has a chance of earning a college scholarship or even playing professional basketball just like Stephen Curry. Follow these tips and techniques and your shot will be looking like Stephen Curry in no time!

Your goal is not to be amazing over night. Work on it every day and over time your shot will be great. Keep practicing and striving for consistency. Make goals and even chart your shots, both in practice and in games. You simply should just have the desire to improve and all will fall into place.

But more than anything, remember to have fun. I started playing basketball, just like I hope you did, to have fun with my friends. When you get better and are able to put more points on the board and have the announcer call your name, it is fun. When you hear the cheerleaders and the fans clapping for your shots, it is fun. Make sure that you keep basketball fun and your growth and development will be exciting!

Good luck on your new shot and now you have the tools to shoot better than Stephen Curry!

For further coaching send an email to onlinebasketballcoaching@gmail.com to receive a special bonus.

Manufactured by Amazon.ca
Acheson, AB